Standards

Controversial Issues in Education

Tracking: Conflicts and Resolutions
Character Education: Controversy and Consensus
Standards: From Policy to Practice

Standards

From Policy to Practice

Anne Turnbaugh Lockwood

CORWIN PRESS, INC.
A Sage Publications Company
Thousand Oaks, California

For information:

Corwin Press, Inc.
A Sage Publications Company
2455 Teller Road
Thousand Oaks, California 91320
E-mail: order@corwinpress.com

SAGE Publications Ltd.
6 Bonhill Street
London EC2A 4PU
United Kingdom

SAGE Publications India Pvt. Ltd.
M-32 Market
Greater Kailash I
New Delhi 110 048 India

Printed in the United States of America

Library of Congress Cataloging-in-Publication Data

Lockwood, Anne Turnbaugh.
   Standards: From policy to practice / Anne Turnbaugh Lockwood.
      p.   cm. — (Controversial issues in education)
   Includes bibliographical references.
   ISBN 0-8039-6622-9 (cloth : acid-free paper)
   ISBN 0-8039-6270-3 (pbk. : acid-free paper)
   1. Education—Standards—United States.   2. Mathematics—Study and
teaching—Standards—United States.   3. Language
arts—Standards—United States.   I. Title.   II. Series.
LB3060.83 .L63   1998
379.1′58′0973—ddc21   98-25309

This book is printed on acid-free paper.

98 99 00 01 02 03 10 9 8 7 6 5 4 3 2 1

Corwin Press Production Editor: S. Marlene Head
Editorial Assistant: Kristen L. Gibson
Typesetter: Andrea D. Swanson
Cover Designer: Marcia M. Rosenburg

Contents

About the Author

Anne Turnbaugh Lockwood, an education writer and analyst, is an Honorary Fellow in the Department of Curriculum and Instruction, University of Wisconsin–Madison. The author of numerous reports, monographs, and articles on education, she is also the author of the following books: *Tracking: Conflicts and Resolutions* (Corwin Press, 1996), *Character Education: Controversy and Consensus* (Corwin Press, 1997), and *Conversations With Educational Leaders: Contemporary Viewpoints on Education in America* (State University of New York Press, 1997).

Lockwood has written and developed a wide variety of publications for organizations that include the North Central Regional Educational Laboratory, the Hispanic Dropout Project of the U.S. Department of Education, the U.S. Department of Education's Office of Bilingual Education and Minority Language Affairs, and the U.S. Department of Education's Office of Educational Research and Improvement. At the University of Wisconsin, she developed two nationally respected publications programs for the National Center on Effective Secondary Schools and the National Center for Effective Schools, respectively. Her work has been recognized by the American Educational Research Association Interpretive Scholarship Award and by the University of Wisconsin's School of Education.

Introduction:
The Case for Standards

Any educator, school board member, or parent might admit to some initial surprise once told that the nation's schools need more rigorous standards for what students learn and how well they learn it—although, at a superficial level, they probably would not argue with the notion. However, they might wonder: Don't grades and test scores already provide some measure of how well students achieve? Why are new standards for content and performance really necessary? What will my child or student learn—and how necessary is this knowledge to his or her future?

Recent test results from the Third International Mathematics and Science Study (TIMSS), released in 1998 by the National Center for Education Statistics (NCES), reveal the academic performance of U.S. 12th graders to be among the lowest of the participating countries in mathematics and science, general knowledge, physics, and advanced mathematics (NCES, 1998).

These and other discouraging test scores, combined with scores of equally dismal reports, have documented that American education needs significant improvement in comparison to the other developed nations of the world (Boyer, 1983; Carnegie Forum on Education, 1986; Holmes Group, 1986; National Commission for Excellence in Teacher Education, 1985; National Commission on Excellence in Education, 1983).

But even concerned individuals who are convinced that academic standards for content and performance need an infusion of rigor could be overwhelmed by the sheer complexity and proliferation of the standards movement. When they discover that there are many standards-based reforms synthesized under the general heading of "standards"—such as standards for teacher professional development, preservice training for teachers, and standards for the delivery of education to students (opportunity-to-learn standards)—they understandably could be confused. Even the most dedicated teacher or school principal could view the task of implementing content and performance standards as too massive and mysterious, or simply unnecessary—yet another fleeting educational trend.

Just as educators and policymakers could be daunted by the size and scope of standards-based reforms, they could become totally perplexed by the sheer array and complexity of different standards that have been developed by national professional organizations in their respective content areas. To date, standards either have been developed or are being developed in mathematics, science, history (world and U.S.), English/language arts, the arts, civics, economics, foreign language, teaching English to students of other languages (ESL), geography, social studies, health, physical education, technology, behavioral studies, and life skills (Kendall & Marzano, 1997). These standards often overlap or contend with each other, as can be seen by the presence of standards for social studies, history, economics, civics, and geography.

At the same time, the logic that underpins the notion of more challenging and specific standards for what students learn and how well they learn might seem compelling. For those educators and interested observers who were steeled to do battle in the nation's schools by the rhetoric of *A Nation at Risk* (National Commission on Excellence in Education, 1984), higher and more specific standards sound like a positive development. Even less alarmed—and informed—individuals would not argue that they would like to see their children's education become both more demanding and more connected to their preparation for future education and the world of work. But when confronted with the hard work of taking standards developed by a plethora of national professional organizations and reworking them to suit the needs of states and local communities, educators face a much thornier task. What are some questions that educators and community members should consider and confront as they engage in this reform?

In this book, I examine the reflections and experiences of educational leaders who have been pioneers in the standards movement—whether they have worked at the national or local level—focusing solely on content and performance standards. I introduce the topic—and these leaders—with a brief overview of some of the most hotly debated questions that swirl around the topic of standards for content and performance.

Some of the most difficult questions related to content and performance standards include the following:

- Why do we need such standards?
- What should students learn, and in what manner?
- How should standards be set, and by whom?
- Are these standards solely for the college bound, or are all students held to equally high expectations?
- How should student performance on content standards be assessed?
- What implications do standards for content and performance have for both schools and teachers?

Why are standards for content and performance necessary? Proponents of standards for content and performance believe that whatever de facto standards exist in public schools are not sufficient. They point to the ways in which student achievement lags behind that of other nations, expressing concern that American students fall far short of the mark (Ravitch, 1995; Smith, Fuhrman, & O'Day, 1994). Such deficient performance, they argue, holds serious consequences for the future economic productivity of the United States.

These individuals and organizations see standards as a type of powerful organizer that will help affect systemic reform—a catalyst for significant change that will align different educational components, such as curriculum materials, assessments, textbooks, teacher professional development, teacher preservice, and the actual content of what students learn. Based on the hypothesis that it is not only possible, but desirable, to reach a common core of valued knowledge that teachers should teach and students should learn, advocates of standards point to the ways in which the curriculum varies state to state, district to district, and sometimes school to school.

These advocates critique the lack of uniformity in education that students receive in the United States, pointing out that it is not only possible but likely that students who move state to state or even district to district receive and participate in an education of strikingly different content and quality than the education previously encountered. Teachers may experience the same when moving from district to district or state to state: Previously rigorous standards may not hold, mandated content may differ dramatically, and even graduation requirements in differing states may be disparate. In short, graduating from high school may not mean the same thing nationwide—and, in fact, probably doesn't.

What do standards for content and performance offer? The vision of reformers who believe in standards-based education is that the curriculum will be arranged around a consensually agreed-upon core body of knowledge that is determined by states and local communities. This body of knowledge will prepare students for the demands of a technologically sophisticated society and will address the needs of employers who complain of entry-level workers who are illiterate and who lack even the most basic skills. Simultaneously, this core body of knowledge will prepare students to go beyond rote memorization and drill to new skills that reformers agree are imperative in the next century's workforce: problem solving, analysis, and the ability to work cooperatively.

At the same time, simply arriving upon core standards for content—which in itself is politically contentious and difficult—is only the beginning of a complicated, lengthy, and laborious process. To teach to these new standards, teachers will also need to assume new competencies. Because their teacher preservice education most likely did not equip them to teach in this way, they need an infusion of professional development that is standards based, practical, and constructivist. Teachers need professional development that extends beyond exhortations to highly practical strategies that they can use in their classrooms with new content. They need the opportunity to observe other teachers working with standards-based curricula, and they require ample occasions to receive nonthreatening feedback as they grapple with new curriculum materials, classroom activities, and assessments.

What should students learn? In what manner? Who decides? Arriving at a consensually agreed-upon core body of knowledge is problematic at best. The American tradition of education demands local control of public schools, with considerable layperson input into the educational process. Therefore, some common, nationally prescribed core curriculum is not practical.

The task of determining a core body of knowledge also has to be realized in the context of a democracy. Other countries have centralized control over education and can prescribe what will be taught and in what manner. However, in the United States a long-standing tradition of local control over public education with ample layperson input into the educational process means that very different points of view have to be solicited and consensus reached before standards in just one content area can be developed.

In what ways do standards for content and performance respect and further the American commitment to equity in education—as well as excellence? Are these standards solely for the college bound, or are all students held to equally high expectations? Critics and advocates of content and performance standards entertain a wide variety of concerns (Apple, 1993; Berliner & Biddle, 1996; Meier, 1989). They caution that adequate provisions may not be made in either standards or assessments matched to the standards for nontraditional student populations. They question whether these standards actually hold all students to high expectations and academic goals or, instead, assume a certain previous educational experience and college-bound aspirations. Or they worry that some students, predominantly minority children, who are assigned to low-track classes from which there is little upward movement will receive a lower-tier education that does not reflect the new standards.

How should student performance on content standards be assessed? Advocates of standards for content and performance appear to agree that new forms of assessment are necessary to measure student performance, including so-called authentic forms of assessment that extend beyond the standard multiple-choice and short-answer format (Smith, Stevenson, & Li, 1998). They also argue that it is necessary to reach individual scores for each student's performance so that the student, his or her family, and school staff can make educated comparisons about his or her performance compared to the rest of the students in the grade, in other schools, and in other states. This information, they contend, will aid teachers and other school staff in the refinements necessary to adjust the curriculum and other components of the educational experience so that student performance can be boosted.

Of course, new forms of assessment without corresponding changes in content will be meaningless. Some advocates have called for voluntary national tests, in which districts would participate of their own volition. The government would not access or use test results, but federal resources would be committed to the development of these tests, which would be based on the National Assessment of Educational Progress (NAEP). Unlike NAEP's measures, however, students in fourth-grade reading and eighth-grade mathematics—the levels and content areas considered "gateways" to more sophisticated knowledge—would be assessed on a combination of multiple-choice, short-answer, and essay questions. Each student would receive an individual score; these scores conceivably could be accessed through the World Wide Web by school personnel and parents. To advocates of content and performance standards, this additional layer of assessment will help propel the standards movement and ensure its success (Smith et al., 1998).

What implications do content and performance standards raise for teachers and other school staff—as well as for schools? Certainly, the notion of transforming multiple curricula in different content areas to reflect a common core of knowledge—with assessments aligned to this core of knowledge—will require different skills from teachers. It will also demand that the entire system align itself to support teachers as they work with standards-based curricula and assessments.

Teachers will be ineffective without solid, standards-based materials and texts. Although some textbook publishers are developing materials to match some of the standards developed by national professional organizations—such as the National Council of Teachers of Mathematics—either there is little movement in other content areas or materials are being developed that do not align with existing standards. The message to educators is "Buyer, beware."

The same is true for professional development. As the experiences related by the practitioners in this book illustrate, professional development that is standards based must fill the needs of teachers. It must be concrete and practical, yet motivational. It must be supplemented with the curriculum materials and texts mentioned above so that teachers do not need to endlessly invent their own materials. Some examples of substantive professional development include the use of demonstration teachers who both field-test and provide feedback as teachers work with new curricula; focus groups that deal with teachers' experiences with standards-based curricula, materials, and assessments; and a constructivist approach to professional development that builds upon what teachers already do and know, rather than insisting that they start over.

Professional development is also necessary for school leaders. For administrators to argue persuasively for standards-based curricula in their schools and districts—as well as standards-based assessments—they need to fully understand and participate in any standards development effort under way. Administrators also are the link between community members, parents, and the schools, and they need to embrace standards-based teaching and testing in order for it to succeed as part of the school's or district's comprehensive effort to educate all children.

What happens if schools and staff do not achieve the desired results with standards-based curricula? Some advocates of standards argue for a high-stakes approach to standards implementation that would hold teachers and other school staff accountable for student performance. Others believe a low-stakes approach that lessens teacher accountability is preferable. However, few would argue that a high-stakes approach will be the most effective in mobilizing school staff, although it opens the possibility for dissension within schools, districts, and communities.

Advocates of a high-stakes approach to implementing standards for content and performance typically hold that teachers and other staff need opportunities to improve, including ample professional development. But if student performance does not improve after some period of time, typically a few years, these advocates believe that school reconstitution or other sanctions are justifiable.

An earlier approach could be provided by progressive institutions of teacher education that move to match their own curricula for prospective teachers with new content standards for students. This type of alignment, endorsed by advocates of standards, would infuse the system with a core group of new teachers trained to teach with methods and strategies compatible with the standards movement. They would understand standards-based assessments and teach appropriately "to the test." It is also possible that they would help inform the existing teacher workforce, particularly in the presence of standards-based professional development, and form a critical mass that would help convince other, more experienced teachers that a move to standards-based instruction and curriculum is desirable.

Of course, implications for teacher unions exist as well. If teachers are to be held to new standards of accountability linked to how well students perform on standards-based assessments, unions will balance the degree of protection they afford their members with the need to hold teachers accountable for educational results.

In this volume, my intent is to present the reflections and experiences of educational figures who have pioneered some aspect of standards for content and performance. My hope is that through their words—and an increased awareness of the complexity of issues that surround this topic—practitioners and prospective school staff will extend their knowledge and inform their existing practice.

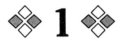

1

Standards in the Context of Democracy: Thomas A. Romberg

Thomas A. Romberg is the Sears Roebuck Foundation–Bascom Professor in Education at the University of Wisconsin–Madison. From 1988 to 1996, he was Director of the National Center for Research in Mathematical Sciences Education, and currently, he is the Director of the National Center for Improving Student Learning and Achievement in Mathematics and Science for the U.S. Department of Education. He is also the Principal Investigator on the NSF-funded curriculum project, Mathematics in Context, a Connected Curriculum for Grades 5-8, *and on the NSF-funded Longitudinal/Cross Sectional Study of the Impact of Mathematics in Context on Student Mathematical Performance.*

Romberg has a long history of involvement with mathematics curriculum reform, including work in the 1960s with the School Mathematics Study Group, in the 1970s with Developing Mathematical Processes, and in the 1980s as chair of two commissions—School Mathematics: Options for the 1990s (U.S. Department of Education) and Curriculum and Evaluation Standards for School Mathematics (National Council of Teachers of Mathematics). In the 1990s, he served as chair of the Assessment Standards for School Mathematics (National Council of Teachers of Mathematics). For his work on the Curriculum and Evaluation Standards Commission, the American Educational Research Association gave him both its Interpretive Scholarship and its Professional Service awards in 1991.

Romberg is internationally well known for his study and involvement with mathematics curriculum reform efforts. He has had fellowships to both Australia and Russia; he has examined current work in England, Australia, the Netherlands, Russia, Sweden, Norway, Germany, Spain, Japan, and Venezuela; and he is currently collaborating with scholars at the University of Utrecht.

Although any education reform unfolds with public expectations for positive outcomes, these hopes easily can be inflated by unrealistic optimism, tempered by prudence, or deflated by pessimism. Which expectations of the national standards movement are realistic? How much should educators, policymakers, and members of the general public expect from this reform?

The answers to these questions, Romberg believes, can be found in the democratic process and the laborious pace of change it requires. Achieving lasting educational change, he points out, is a much more ambitious endeavor than in other countries, where change frequently can be dictated by a central ministry of education, and schools follow national edicts.

Education reform in the United States, he adds, is made even more intricate because of a lack of cohesive national experience with long-term planning, as well as a history of impatience with the pace of education innovation.

"In this country, our planning is very much in the short term," Romberg begins—which, he adds, is amply illustrated by the rapid turnover of public elected officials.

Brief planning periods, pressured by eagerness for dramatically positive results, can also be accompanied by a type of ill-founded optimism that big changes can occur in short periods of time. "When a president is elected, it is for a 4-year term," he says. "Senators get a 6-year term; congressmen 2 years. School board members typically serve a 2-year term.

"The elective process," he adds, "is such that it almost demands short-term planning without serious thought to long-term planning."

As a result, unrealistic expectations for positive change abound, Romberg believes, and these expectations easily spill over into the arena of education. The results can be disappointment at the least and, more profoundly, a sense of disillusionment. This becomes problematic when education reformers try to fit their agenda to public values and norms, knowing that any reform must have a realistic timeline before results can be realized.

Realism and Reform

"Being realistic about reform," Romberg says, "means having a vision that can be accomplished over several years. The next step is laying out a plan for what can be achieved this year, next year, in 3 years, and in 5 years."

But in a democracy, this type of realism can be unwieldy, in comparison to other countries. Compared to a country such as Japan, for instance, the United States falters in its willingness to look long-term and set realistic goals, Romberg maintains. "In meetings I had in Japan last year, they spent a lot of time discussing a major change in their mathematics curriculum—a change that will be implemented in 2005. They realize that they won't be ready to implement it until then. Obviously, that's a different system with a whole different set of notions about how to plan, with centralized control rather than local control, and a whole variety of other things that are different from our educational system."

Realistic expectations of any education reform in the United States are further confounded by the political nature of American schooling and by long-standing tension between locally held values and loftier national goals. "What's realistic here?" Romberg asks rhetorically. "We argued that the *NCTM Standards* be used as background documents for planning at the state and local levels. This hasn't turned out to be totally what we planned.

"States are working on their standards, but it will be another 10 years before they can give attention to preparing teachers to teach this way, developing curriculum materials that fit, and aligning assessment with standards. Successful long-term planning would involve orchestrating all of these factors in tandem."

Reformers' Expectations
and the Reality of Reform

What about the expectations of reformers who have spear-
headed the national standards movement? To what extent have
their plans been followed? Have there been egregious surprises as
they have watched states and communities either use the *NCTM
Standards* or develop their own?

The wake of the *NCTM Standards* has not been exactly what the
Standards developers anticipated, Romberg says, although the developers are gratified that the documents have springboarded
much state and local action. As one example, the authors called for
a year of national dialogue that didn't occur. Somewhat paradoxi-
cally, local dialogue has flourished instead.

"Most of the short-term changes have been positive," he adds.
"States are developing new assessments and new standards. New
text materials are coming out and teacher education programs are
changing. They are not all aligned with the same vision, but they
reflect the considerable debate that is occurring."

But reformers at the national level can also experience frustration as states and communities spend large amounts of time and
money to develop their own standards—which may or may not
reflect the care and intellectual deliberation given to the development of standards at the national level. In some cases, these efforts
can leave the national standards effort open to criticism precisely
because state or local efforts aren't faithful to the national standards and thus do not achieve the desired results.

California is an example of a state that announced it was adhering
to the national framework, Romberg notes, but actually offered its
teachers a menu that was quite different. "California established its
framework in 1992 and said it followed the *NCTM Standards.* But
if we look at the actual documents that were developed, we see
very little reflection of the *Standards.* Instead, the emphasis is much
more on pedagogy and not on the content of mathematics as it was
emphasized in the *Standards.* As one example, there is a great deal
of emphasis on working on projects in groups."

This emphasis on structure and process may have been well-
intentioned, but it does not further the cause of the *NCTM Standards* or any carefully developed national framework of standards, he

says. "In the California situation, the projects that students worked on may have been interesting, but stringing half a dozen of them together to form a curriculum didn't necessarily teach them very much about mathematics."

California's experience, he adds, illustrates the complexities of reform based on a national framework. "Sometimes," Romberg reflects with irony, "it is frightening when people take you seriously."

What can easily happen, he adds, is that an idea from a national framework will achieve instant popularity without thoughtful discussion of its complexities and how they should relate to curriculum and pedagogy. Later, the reformers will be criticized because a state developed a curriculum that is "soft" or devoid of adequate content in mathematics.

"Textbook publishers and school staff follow," he explains, "but if the teachers who have changed their practice actually had better materials to work with, the kinds of outcomes we wanted would be easier to achieve."

To ensure quality control, the *NCTM Standards* developers wanted to establish criteria for curriculum materials to ensure that the materials met the *Standards* if the developers made that claim. "We wanted to put a stamp of approval on certain materials, just as the American Dental Association does on toothpaste," Romberg says.

"Unfortunately, for a variety of reasons, NCTM decided not to do that. No one has dealt with the problem of making judgments about whether or not textbooks, teacher training programs, or tests actually meet the *Standards*. As a result, any publisher can claim that its materials meet the *Standards*."

Again, negative feedback affects the reformers and the national movement, he points out. "Critics can easily say that the lack of results is due to the *Standards* rather than the materials that schools have available to work with, especially when all sorts of companies and individuals claim their products are congruent with the Standards."

Local Development of World-Class Standards

There is much rhetoric about developing "world-class" standards, but what does the term actually mean? Is it an oxymoron for local communities to endeavor to develop world-class standards?

"World class is a political term," Romberg says, "that grew out of the international comparisons. Politicians argue that we should be first in the world in achievement, without describing what that means. It is a statement of political rhetoric without substance.

"What does it really mean?" he asks. "For many people, it means that our students will score near the top on any tests that they take. But we are not in a position to dictate to schools the kinds of social conditions that exist in other countries that produce that type of high achievement. For example, no one argues that we should change the licensing of teachers or the staffing of schools."

The gap between political rhetoric and high standards in a democracy is actually a deep and difficult-to-bridge chasm, Romberg says. "The rest of the world assumes that only 20 to 25 percent of its students will go to college. We assume that everyone has the right to go to college.

"Our assumption means that there is really only one high school program: college prep. If you're not in that, you don't have anything sensible to do."

The meaning of college in the United States also differs from its meaning in other countries, Romberg points out. "In this country, college can be something you fall into because you don't know what else to do. In other countries, you are admitted to a college to study something specific, such as mathematics or engineering or law."

But pragmatism must color the aspirations of reformers and the general public alike, he believes. "The frustrating part for people like me and others involved in reform is that frequently we don't consider those cultural components of education. We don't fully recognize the vision and ideas that have taken a long time to develop. The kind of change we want won't happen overnight."

National Standards and Local Values

Given the ways in which the standards movement is mushrooming in most states—along with the local imprimatur that many communities want to place on any standards effort—to what extent is there danger that there may be such a proliferation of standards that they become meaningless? Is the tension between locally developed and national standards sufficient to capsize and swamp the standards movement entirely?

"In the *NCTM Standards*," Romberg replies, "we tried to convey intellectually based arguments about what is happening in the discipline of mathematics along with what we know about learning and what other countries do when they teach mathematics.

"But if a local community doesn't believe this is what they want their children to learn, it is their right to set their standards accordingly. For example, in one school district I visited recently, teaching the slide rule was still important, although no one uses it anymore."

This example of dissonance between some local commitments and national standards is particularly key, he says. "It is a disservice to our children not to keep mathematics up to date," he emphasizes, "and that was a big part of the *NCTM Standards*. For example, we need to include in our curriculum a fair amount of statistics and the use of technology."

The problem with change, Romberg maintains, often occurs when the power of personal experience collides with innovation and reform. "When schools begin to advocate things that are different from what parents learned and from what they saw school to mean, we no longer are engaged in an intellectual debate. Instead, what is taught and how it is taught becomes a question of values."

These values vary community-to-community, state-to-state, and could conceivably neutralize the national standards effort—which seeks some kind of uniform high standards nationwide. "Every state has its own set of beliefs about what it thinks is important in each content area," Romberg explains. "In mathematics, there is a common element that grew up in the 1930s and '40s: Eight years of arithmetic, a year of algebra, and a year of geometry. However, the 11th- and 12th-grade courses vary dramatically state-to-state, district-to-district. Non-college-bound courses vary as well. States also differ on whether they offer a course in statistics. So the criteria, even in mathematics, tend to be quite different historically."

This state-by-state diversity means that students who move frequently may receive a cobbled-together education of varying quality—or else be held to different standards in one district than in another. Again, this reflects the long-standing belief in local control, Romberg says, even though it runs counter to the belief that national standards can provide a core set of expectations that students should meet, no matter where they live.

National Standards and
Voluntary National Tests

To many reformers, national standards are linked with a voluntary national testing system that would set benchmarks for student performance at particular grade levels. Will voluntary national tests—despite the stormy political debate they have endured—take root in the American educational landscape?

Romberg first points out the huge set of hurdles that any developers of voluntary national tests would have to overcome. "The idea behind the tests is that we ought to be able to demonstrate that all of our students can read by the end of the third grade. That is a very nice political statement, but what does it mean to have them learn how to read?

"The same holds true for arithmetic, algebra, and geometry by the end of eighth grade, because that is when the transition to high school occurs and they are tracked into various classes."

The rhetoric is legitimate, Romberg believes, but the difficulties are almost insurmountable. "Once we start talking about any particular test, whether it is in reading or mathematics, we need to realize it is constrained by the political realities of the American education system. Who is going to volunteer to take the test? How are the results going to be used? Will it be high-stakes testing, in which decisions are made about which programs kids get into and what schools they go to in the future? Will it be low-stakes testing, where kids learn to fill in the bubbles on the test? And if it's not high stakes, why bother?"

There are even more constraints that may quash these tests before they're developed, he adds. "Politicians don't know a great deal about testing. They don't want to spend the money to produce a good test. Instead, they would like to use items from other tests developed for other purposes. That creates another set of problems."

Economy, he believes, does not always further educational productivity. "There are currently studies under way of strategies to link some test items to other test items. But group indicators aren't designed to deal with individual students. And group indicators certainly aren't diagnostic."

School Staff and Standards

When school staff either engage in the development of standards or work from guidelines such as the *NCTM Standards*, which school staff should be involved in the process? Are there ways to select individuals that will both maximize the return and minimize political conflicts?

"Clearly," Romberg replies, "you want people who are concerned about improving education. You want to include people with different views, because if those views are not shared in the early planning stages, there will be difficulties later. After all, we encourage dissent in this country. There are few issues about which there is broad consensus."

Above all, he believes that school staff, reformers, and policymakers need to join together in a new sense of realism and optimism that can inform their educational decisions. "How do we produce change in a democratic system?" Romberg asks. "We have a society that values individual local control of education. We worry about equality of educational opportunity for our students; our students have huge differences in their opportunities to learn and in the resources and support that is available.

"We must not," he emphasizes, "be overwhelmed with frustration but press on for positive results."

Standards-Based Mathematics
Reform in Practice:
Diane J. Briars

Diane J. Briars is Mathematics Curriculum Consultant in the Office of Curriculum, Instruction and Assessment of the Pittsburgh Public Schools, and Co-director of PRIME, the Pittsburgh Reform in Mathematics Education Project. She is responsible for providing technical assistance on all aspects of the K-12 mathematics program for the Pittsburgh Public Schools, including curriculum and assessment development, professional development, and the development of special programs. She also is Director of the Assessment Communities of Teachers Project (in conjunction with the Urban Mathematics Collaboratives and EDC), which supports middle school teachers in Pittsburgh and five other urban districts (Dayton, Memphis, Milwaukee, San Diego, and San Francisco) as they learn to use various assessment tools in their classrooms.

At the national level, Briars is involved in initiatives in mathematics education. She was Co-Chairperson of the Purposes Working Group for the National Council of Teachers of Mathematics (NCTM) Assessment Standards for School Mathematics and a member of the working group that drafted the evaluation section of the NCTM Curriculum and Evaluation Standards for School Mathematics. She is a former Director of the National Council of Teachers of Mathematics.

Currently, she also is a Trustee of the College Board; a member of the NSF Advisory Committee for Education and Human Resources; and a member of the Mathematics Advisory Committee of the New Standards Project, a national initiative to improve educa-

*tion through the development of an examination system centered
around students' performance, projects, and portfolios.*

W hen the Pittsburgh Public Schools began its aggressive, standards-based mathematics curriculum reform in the 1990s,
hope was abundant. A spirit of optimism and efficacy permeated the
district; mathematics specialists approached their task with respect
for its enormity but were not daunted by potential obstacles.

But as the 1990s unfurled, they were accompanied by dramatic
district administrative changes, draconian budget cuts, and
districtwide restructuring—all of which changed the countenance
of reform in the district. The division of mathematics was elimi-
nated, as was a central office budget dedicated to mathematics.
District funds for professional development were sharply reduced,
as were the number of professional development days.

As a result, one might expect that standards-based mathematics reform in the Pittsburgh Public Schools ground to a halt, sty-
mied by forces bigger than the reform itself. But although the
reform has been affected dramatically by the systemic change occurring around it, Briars argues that surprising progress has been
made.

"While engaged in its restructuring," she recollects, "the district began some overall strategic planning. As a part of this, it
made a strong commitment to standards-based instruction.

"The district also became involved in the New Standards
Project developed by Lauren Resnick and Marc Tucker.[1] As a result
of that involvement, we began working with the New Standards
performance-based assessments in mathematics, which were
based on the content standards developed by the National Council
of Teachers of Mathematics."

Briars is careful to emphasize that no one factor is the fulcrum
upon which Pittsburgh's comprehensive mathematics reform is poised.
Instead, a complex interaction of standards-based curriculum
materials, sufficient and practical professional development, and

an accountability piece that school leaders take seriously all must be in place to nudge reform forward.

The assessments developed by the New Standards Project have already influenced the reception of new curriculum materials because they are linked to the standards around which these materials revolve. Briars explains, "Resnick and Tucker began their work in 1991, creating benchmark exams similar to those in Europe, where there is an examination system with clear accountability. They initially recruited 22 states and six school districts as partners. Pittsburgh was one of the six school districts."

The New Standards Project developed an exam in mathematics that would contain both a reference exam and a portfolio piece. "To date, only the reference exam is functional," Briars says. "These exams are offered at 4th, 8th, and 10th or 11th grades. The results are standards based, meaning that student achievement is based on how well they measure up to performance standards in mathematics skills, concepts, and problem solving." In fact, Briars contends, one of the chief benefits of such assessment is the fact that students are compared against a standard, not against other students.

Standards-Based Instructional Materials

But standards-based assessments alone—without robust, standards-based instructional materials—would not produce the necessary results. Pittsburgh has an intricate adoption procedure for mathematics curriculum materials that relies on teachers who are willing to pilot new materials in their classrooms over a period of time.

"As a result of our pilots, we adopted a program called Everyday Mathematics at the elementary levels, K-5," Briars reports. "We phased in this program grade by grade. This year, we are working with Everyday Mathematics at the fourth grade; fifth grade will be implemented next year."

In middle school, the district adopted a program called Connected Mathematics. As Briars explains, "We've progressed with it to the seventh grade this year. Next year, we'll be implementing the program at the eighth grade."

At the high school level, a final decision on instructional materials has not been made. "We're piloting a couple of programs," she notes, "one of which is Core Plus, an integrated algebra/geometry 3-year program. We're also piloting another set of materials out of California that is more traditional in approach."

The implementation of these new materials could not have occurred without a local systemic change grant from the National Science Foundation (NSF), Briars notes, particularly when professional development in the district suffered large cuts.

Standards-Based Professional Development

"We provide a combination of workshops and in-class demonstration teachers who support teachers in their classrooms while they are learning to use the materials. These demonstration teachers provide collegial support as well as more structured forms of support, particularly at the middle level."

At the middle school level, demonstration teachers go into classrooms to work with an individual teacher for a specified period of time, such as 3 weeks. "These demonstration teachers teach the period while the regular classroom teacher observes," Briars explains. "The next step is for the demonstration teacher to observe the classroom teacher in a subsequent period and offer feedback."

Any anxiety the classroom teacher might experience is alleviated by the fact that the demonstration teacher does not represent any type of accountability measure. "The demonstration teacher never documents the classroom teacher's performance, never provides data that could support an unsatisfactory rating. But the demonstration teacher definitely provides support and help with the planning."

All staff development, Briars explains, is intensely practical and hands-on—a deliberate focus that eschews the general and motivational to deliver to teachers what they most need to change their instructional practices. "Our initial responsibility is to enable teachers to teach the new instructional material," she notes. "At the middle school level, our professional development for the first year and a half means that we go through each of the units. I'm very serious when I say this. We actually go through each unit and look at the problems, look at the homework, talk about the intent of the problems, how to do them, whatever teachers need.

"We do the same thing at the elementary level. This year, for our fourth-grade implementation, we're doing monthly workshops which focus around one unit respectively. We also do summer workshops that last a week. Their focus is to provide an overview of the material. We spend the rest of that time going through the unit so that teachers are prepared to teach the first few months of school."

She emphasizes, "Initially, our professional development is very concrete. We also deal with assessment as we go along. What do you assess? How do you do it? Finally, we provide a lot of support around what is working for teachers, what is clearly not working, what dilemmas they have encountered, what solutions they have found to those dilemmas—with an emphasis on collegial support and sharing of experiences."

But over time, professional development expands to focus on other issues, she adds, including increasing teachers' overall knowledge and understanding of mathematics.

Teachers greet this professional development with enthusiasm, Briars says, because they see a clear application for the content in their classrooms. "At the beginning, we thought we would work in larger pieces and move further away from the material. We couldn't. Teachers want the nitty-gritty. They want us to demonstrate a lesson. It also was helpful that we could pilot these new instructional materials. Our demonstration teachers had enormous credibility with classroom teachers because they had taught the materials already."

Demonstration teachers also have an expanded role that includes outreach to both parents and building-level administrators. "They conduct many parent-teacher meetings as well as talk to administrators about the goals for the instruction," Briars adds.

Expectations and Standards

From her perspective as a reform agent in a large urban district with its share of financial hardship, how much does Briars believe the standards movement can deliver? What outcomes should the public expect?

"In mathematics," she responds with cautious optimism, "we should expect that we can get all students to achieve at much higher levels. This is a reasonable expectation, and I think we can accomplish it. Not only do we now have standards, but we have new instructional materials based on those standards that are dramatically different from what we have used in the past. We also have assessments that are very different from the past. Finally, more money for professional development is available in mathematics than in some other content areas."

At minimum, Briars believes that it is reasonable to expect that high school graduates who have received a standards-based mathematics education will be better prepared to deal with everyday uses of math. "Even if high school doesn't change much," she adds, "if we dramatically change elementary and middle school, we'll do a lot to change what people know and understand about mathematics."

Providing a rich elementary and middle school experience in mathematics, she suggests, also can armor students for college and their futures whether or not high school mathematics changes sufficiently. "Kids who have gone through a good elementary and middle school program come out with a better number sense, a much better understanding of mathematics and number concepts. They understand measurement and know how to do it. Also, since there is a heightened emphasis on algebraic thinking in the elementary and middle school programs, they will have a better understanding of variables. They will have better preparation in geometry and a more sophisticated spatial sense."

High Schools and the Pace of Change

What about high schools and the slow pace of change? Why would mathematics teachers at the high school level be especially reluctant to abandon traditional practices?

The answer, Briar believes, is more complex than the usual belief that high school teachers are simply more resistant to change because of the structure within which instruction is delivered. "High school teachers really believe that mathematics is the manipulation of symbols," she says. "They don't see some of the other content as equally important."

Feedback from college mathematics professors who insist that calculators cannot be used in their classes only fuels this resistance, she adds. "Many high school teachers say that they want to do the best for kids—but they may not necessarily want to do the best for all kids. It's not so much that they don't want to change as it is a set of beliefs about mathematics combined with what they hear from people above them who will eventually work with the students they teach."

These teachers also entertain skepticism about reform, she notes, based on their observations that their current students have not shown dramatic gains in achievement. "They say 'The kids are still coming to us just like they always have.' But that's because our students haven't gone through a complete reformed program yet," Briars says. "That should change once they get students who have had that experience."

The Pace of Standards-Based Reform

Although she remains an optimist about standards-based mathematics reform, Briars etches a fine line between realistic and unrealistic expectations for what it can accomplish—a particularly critical distinction when people are buoyed by the belief that immediate results are possible. "I expect to see some differences 3 years from now," she notes, "based on the fact that 2 years from now we will have the first cohort of students entering high school who have gone all the way through Connected Mathematics. Will they be radically different? Some of them will be, but not all of them, because we will not have experienced total implementation of Connected Mathematics.

"It's a long, long process," she cautions. "When you have a huge system, everyone doesn't implement changes the way they should. Changes are much slower than people can accept. There are also some things that reform will not change."

Among those, Briars indicts the conditions in which many students live, including persistent, debilitating poverty—but she also emphasizes the need to provide more integrated services in their support than most large school systems currently extend. "Many of our students could do more in school but need more support, more imaginative and dramatic responses to their lives outside school. As just one example, schools need to become community centers for these students. Mathematics reform alone is not going to accomplish everything."

She points to some schools that have been developed in Chicago. "As one example, they have a school that runs from 6 a.m. to 8 p.m. The students receive all three meals at school, do their homework at school, and only go home to sleep. There is a dramatic change in achievement in schools such as these because they are dealing with the problems students bring with them in a much more substantial way."

Briars emphasizes, "If we want to get really powerful results, we have to do other things powerfully as well."

Assessment and Accountability

One forceful step has been the positioning of the New Standards reference exam in mathematics as a critical component of accountability for building principals. "In the fall of 1997, principals in our district heard for the first time from an official source that the performance assessments would be worth more than the norm-referenced testing that they were used to. They were told to pay attention to these new assessments and work accordingly to support them."

A standards-based curriculum isn't assisted by norm-referenced tests, she points out parenthetically. "As long as you're simply trying to get high norm-referenced test scores, you don't necessarily have to use the new curriculum. But when you look at the new assessments and realize that your instruction has to match what that is measuring, that makes a huge difference."

Seeing the fit between the new instructional materials and the new assessments can be a motivational force that jump-starts the reform, she argues. "You realize there will be a payoff, and it makes you want to teach the new material."

The availability of good materials, Briars underscores, means that realizing the goals of a reform is tangible and possible. "The standards themselves are interesting," she says, "and important to have in place, but what moves us forward are the instructional materials and the assessments."

How do school staff know if new materials are truly standards based and of high quality? Are there ways in which they can guard against the specious claims of some materials developers?

In her response, Briars points to Pittsburgh's lengthy adoption process, which emphasizes in-classroom piloting of new materials. "We've moved to a much more broad-based and lengthy adoption process," she explains. "We pilot all our materials for at least a year before we use them all over the district. We did not," she emphasizes, "ask everyone to try everything. Instead, we find volunteers to work with a program for a period of time to see if it had any impact on students.

"We're trying to set up criteria for adoption that emphasize that the materials we want to use are the materials that work the best with the students."

Pittsburgh also decided against a full-scale K-8 adoption, Briars adds, favoring a more strategic and targeted approach. "For example, we worked just with kindergarten when Everyday Mathematics came out because kindergarten teachers liked it. We went on to work with Grades 1 and 2 as a package."

She adds, "While this means we will not be using materials that are hot off the presses, it does mean that we recognized that new materials won't make a difference unless teachers actually try them in their classrooms."

Assessing Progress

Given the length of time that the Pittsburgh Public Schools have been working to implement standards-based mathematics instruction and assessment, are there particular lessons that inform their ongoing experience? Would the district do anything differently with the benefit of hindsight but the same constraints?

Briars places additional funding for professional development at the top of her list. "We didn't push hard enough to find funding for professional development when we first did our Grade 1 and 2 implementation of Everyday Mathematics. Those teachers, as a result, received a minimum amount of support. I underestimated how resistant teachers would be and how much change was involved."

Since the district has received its local systemic change grant from NSF, she sees a substantive difference. "We were able to support our third-grade teachers from the beginning. We have gone back and provided support for our K-2 teachers, but we are making up for what we didn't provide earlier. As a result, we have had to undo some misconceptions and change negative feelings instead of building positive feelings from the beginning."

Substantial parent and community outreach is another effort that needs to be nurtured at the outset of any reform, she adds. "I would do more systematic parent and public outreach than we were able to do at the beginning," she says. "We are now encountering some parent resistance. Each school does its own workshop for parents, although we will help them with that effort. Currently, we're searching for more money to do more systemic parental outreach, in which we engage parents in understanding what is going on in the program."

At the middle level, monthly meetings help parents know what to expect, she notes, although she points to the need for some informational pieces to go home with students. "It's difficult when you are working with an activity-based program and a math book doesn't go home with the student," she clarifies. "Parents have a difficult time understanding what their children are doing—particularly when it doesn't mesh with their experience."

She also believes that building-level administrators need more support and education than is currently available. "We need to work much more with administrators at the building level as well as associate superintendents. When the district reorganized, there was no longer an opportunity to do mandatory professional development for the principals, and certainly not with administrators at a higher level."

Voluntary professional development targeted to principals, she adds wryly, attracted precisely those school leaders who didn't need it. "The new standards-based assessments, however, are providing a push because they are built into the principals' accountability. People now show up for these sessions, and we relate their professional development back to the curriculum. Many more people want to learn about it."

She is encouraged by the fact that resistance to new materials, new instructional practices, and new forms of assessment is minimal because teachers have been willing to keep the achievement of their students at the forefront. "I certainly will not say that teachers who tried these new materials didn't have difficulty. But by the end of a year of work with a new program, feelings changed. Even some of our resistant teachers were impressed by the way Everyday Mathematics worked for kids. Their own jobs became more difficult, but they could see that their students were learning more."

This ability to distinguish between the challenge of teaching within a comprehensive reform and what is best for students encourages Briars to look optimistically toward the future. "It certainly isn't magic," she says. "But we already see differences between high-implementation schools and low-implementation schools. That leads us to believe that 2 to 3 years from now, we'll see significant results, results that will keep the reform dynamic and responsive to student needs."

Note

1. Lauren Resnick directs the Learning Research and Development Center at the University of Pittsburgh; Marc Tucker directs the National Center on Education and the Economy in Washington, DC.

3

Equity in the Standards Movement: Walter G. Secada

Walter G. Secada is Professor of Curriculum and Instruction at the University of Wisconsin–Madison, where he directs the Region VI Comprehensive Assistance Center, which is funded by the U.S. Department of Education's Office of Elementary and Secondary Education. He also is an Associate Director in the National Center on Improving Student Learning and Achievement in Mathematics and Science. From 1995 to 1996, he directed the Hispanic Dropout Project at the request of Secretary of Education Richard W. Riley. From 1990 to 1995, he was a principal investigator for the Center on Organization and Restructuring of Schools. Secada has also been an Associate Director of the National Center for Research in Mathematical Sciences Education, Director of a training and technical assistance resource center for bilingual education, and an Associate Dean in the School of Education at the University of Wisconsin–Madison.

Over the past 15 years, his scholarly research and teacher development efforts have included equity in education, mathematics education, bilingual education, and reform. Currently, he is studying how children negotiate the ages of 6 to 12; how secondary students reason about mathematics; school change and mathematics reform; and Hispanic dropout prevention.

Expecting the standards movement to deliver massive change without fitting it into the elaborate context of schooling is myopic as well as misguided, Walter Secada believes, and could further stratify educational opportunities for those students traditionally least served by public schools. He says, "If the standards movement interacts with present-day assumptions about how schools should work and is retrofitted to the status quo, little will change."

Simply placing an attractive overlay—one that boasts of new and rigorous standards—over an inequitable structure is only cosmetic, Secada argues. "If we do this with the standards movement," he notes, "we are saying that we are doing something new but we actually are not."

This cautionary note aside, the standards movement could serve a provocative function by encouraging people to think about and act upon critical issues that affect the quality of education for all students. However, Secada warns that any reform must be considered in a much broader and more intricate context.

"With any movement," he points out, "substantive change always depends on how the reform interacts with existing conditions. The standards movement is not something that can be added onto what schools are already doing. Instead, it requires getting rid of dead underbrush and building structures that work."

Standards and Structures

Tracking provides a clear-cut example of a long-lived school structure that needs both scrutiny and action—and the need to hold all students to high standards can help refine or eliminate this practice. "If we look at tracking and decide to have different standards for different tracks," Secada reasons, "then the standards movement becomes little more than a more powerful way of systematically stratifying opportunity."

But a judicious use of standards, if employed to reexamine an existing structure, could enable equity. "If we view the standards as a demand for all kids to achieve at high levels, then we have to ask and answer our own question: How do we do this?"

Secada continues, "Does tracking help all students achieve at high levels? If so, how? Does it mean that I put my best teachers in the low tracks? Do I need to make my tracks more permeable? Or does it mean we wipe tracking from the educational slate altogether and come up with something different?"

The standards movement, if wielded as a flexible and forceful tool, not only can become an impetus for rethinking structures that will promote high achievement for all students, but can also be used to reconfigure available resources. Secada says, "Some people who study school finance are arguing that the only fixed expense in an elementary school is the cost of the principal's salary plus the teachers that allow the school to have a student-teacher ratio of 20 to 1.

"Every other cost," he adds, "comes from the need to provide additional services. This means that we can ask: How should I configure my teaching staff so that the school works most effectively? What additional services do I need? Is hiring a specialist for every need the best way to purchase those services, or are there other options? In other words, the school's additional budget provides discretionary monies with which to buy what is needed to accomplish the work of the school."

Balancing the goal of high achievement for all students with concerns about equity means that low-achieving students are not abandoned in the enthusiasm that surrounds the standards movement. "While we increase the level to which we want students to achieve," Secada emphasizes, "we need to ensure that low-achieving students aren't left even further behind."

Unfortunately, existing school structures work against an equitable application of standards, he argues. "Most arrangements ensure that kids who are at the top get to be in the smallest classes and get the best resources. This is highly problematic. The highest pupil/teacher ratio is provided to the lowest achievers."

If standards are left at the level of rhetoric and admonitions to states and districts to tighten up their demands and raise their academic expectations for students, teachers also could be left behind. "There is considerable rhetoric and policy devoted to the need to restructure schools in massive ways, but not enough attention or resources devoted to professional development," he adds.

As a result, even if school structures shift to accommodate both the standards movement and concerns about equity, it is unrealistic to expect that teachers can alter their practice to fit the new context in which they must work.

"We simply can't get rid of tracks," Secada says, "and expect teachers to change their practice overnight. It's not enough to say that all children can learn—and expect teachers to bring it about without assistance."

Again, piecemeal considerations of school change without sufficient attention to the context of schooling means that even the most well-intentioned efforts may be doomed. "If we try to change the context in which teachers practice their craft knowledge," he points out, "we need to make it possible for teachers and other school personnel to develop new craft knowledge that helps them deal with the new complexity of teaching."

One weakness of the standards movement, Secada believes, is that it has not provided sufficient explicit material to help teachers make standards for content and performance viable for populations that traditionally have been underserved by schools. He says, "Teachers and school personnel who work with these populations need ongoing help."

But there is an inequitable and pervasive irony. "Teachers who work in the suburbs, in relatively privileged positions, are the first to get access to professional development," Secada points out. "But where is the greatest need? Certainly, all teachers need high-quality professional development, but teachers of low-achieving students have a critical need."

Yet another underacknowledged aspect of the standards movement, he suggests, is that it can change the face of achievement. "If we use new forms of assessment," he explains, "kids who are often labeled as low achievers start to look different. When measured on exploratory forms of learning, creative ways of thinking, and open-ended activities—which intrigue many kids—they begin to do better. One of the reasons they score low on traditional forms of assessment is because much of what occurs in the traditional school is uninteresting and does not engage them."

Expecting just the rhetoric of the standards movement to bring about substantive change is foolish, Secada argues, pointing to the long time any educational change requires. "This is a long-term, systematic effort," he says, "because we are talking about changing thousands of schools, hundreds of thousands of teachers and school personnel, and millions of kids. Such change is not done easily."

He adds, "A lot of time, energy, newsprint, and media time is spent talking and not enough time is spent doing. The level of rhetoric far exceeds the level of action."

Local Beliefs, Standards, and Equity

Given the tradition of local control of public schools, it is not impossible that a community might hold inequitable—but carefully disguised—beliefs that reify existing school structures and practices that benefit only those students who are already high achievers. What should educators do if community members urge standards based on values and beliefs that promote inequitable practices?

Secada's response is swift and sure. "Other parents or community members should file a lawsuit," he says tartly. "Equal educational opportunity is the law of the land, a constitutional right. We can argue about how we achieve it. We can argue about its meaning. But if it is clear that a community has inequitable values that they codify in their statements about standards, then the district may be creating separate and unequal practices."

But he believes that adequate outreach and education to community members at the beginning of any standards effort can encourage equitable and rigorous practices. "Educators have an obligation to educate the community. If community members hold certain biases, those need to be exposed, to be made public."

The balance is precarious, however, because educators need to respect the values of a community as long as they are not unfair or prejudicial. "We do need to respect what local community members feel is important," he adds. "One way is to encourage parents to ask themselves: Am I happy with this? Is this right for my kids? And if this is what I want for my kids, would I want it for everyone's kids?"

Those fundamental questions, Secada adds, not only make rhetoric about standards and equity more immediate and tangible, but they also add what he terms "moral anchoring"—a quality sorely needed by any educational reform. "Educators and community members also have a responsibility to educate themselves more broadly. They need to be aware of actions occurring nationally and at the state level in terms of what type of education we are providing our kids. How does this education prepare them to achieve and to aspire to other things?"

Fundamental questions, he points out, include the following: What happens to a community's graduates? How many enter college? How many graduate from college? How high is the drop-out rate? Why is the drop-out rate so high, and what actions can be taken to avert it?

"Answers to these questions," Secada explains, "give a sense of how the community stacks up next to the rest of the state and possibly the country."

He adds, "If our graduates are not aspiring to college, what does that say about us? In other words, if our children are not accomplishing what we want them to accomplish, we need to wonder if we are providing them with an adequate and appropriate education. If we have evidence that makes us content with the quality of education we are providing to all students, then that should be respected as long as it is not biased or inherently inequitable."

Certain programs, such as those provided for students identified as gifted and talented, are difficult to defend. "Why do we provide something special for those students," Secada asks, "and not for others? Can we justify resources for a narrow segment of the population? We need to continually ask ourselves: Why should this special population of children receive a different education that others might profit from as well?"

Tracking is another practice that endures criticism for justifiable reasons, he notes. "No track should be distinguished from another track on the basis of race, gender, or social class," he asserts. "Is it possible to achieve an equitable tracking system, or is that an oxymoron? Is it possible to achieve an equitable gifted-and-talented program? Some would say yes; others would say no. Some would contend that there is something fundamentally inequitable about the fact that schools persist with these practices."

Whatever the program, Secada believes it should look like the total school population. "If people are afraid that a program might become second-rate were its students to represent the whole population, that immediately becomes an indicator that equity is not present," he says. "That becomes a reason to eliminate that program. The concern should not be that if a program is heterogeneous, it no longer has an elite quality."

Achieving Standards and Equity

It is clear that Secada believes that the standards movement can be guided by an overriding concern about whether the education provided to all students is equitable and rigorous. "Sometimes, we view the standards movement as either for or against equity," he adds. "Instead, we need to ask: How can people who are committed to equity in schooling also be committed to high standards for all students—including those who traditionally have been low achievers? What do we have to do to achieve equity and standards for these kids?"

Believing that it is possible, and necessary, to achieve both high standards and equity in educational practices eliminates false dichotomies, he adds. "Most of the time, our thinking on this topic settles into artificially hardened positions with opposing camps throwing sound bites at each other."

Instead, he maintains that the standards movement has not been given adequate time to prove itself. "We have a few sites nationally that are doing interesting things with curriculum," he says, "and also with instruction. There are a few places where forms of assessment are ambitious and differ from what is usually done, but very few places that have high-quality curriculum tied to high-quality teaching tied to high-quality forms of assessment. These sites are well known, which demonstrates how rare they actually are."

Putting a local stamp on the standards movement not only gives educators at the district and building level a sense of ownership but also provides an opportunity for them to engage in a type of reflection and study that is not encouraged by the present system, he adds. "We don't learn unless we do it ourselves," he points out. "The national standards are culminating statements of years of thoughtful reflection, learning, working, and thinking things through. They did not spring fully formed like Athena from the head of Zeus."

Instead, the national standards written by professional organizations in different content areas are summaries, he believes. "Most local districts have not had that experience of reflecting about standards, thinking about what knowledge students need to learn, and then writing standards statements that sum up their beliefs. For that reason, developing local standards serves an important learning function for the people participating in that debate."

In fact, although it may appear unnecessary, Secada believes that local development of standards is necessary to ensure the success of the entire standards movement. "If local districts accept whatever national standards have been developed, the likelihood of changing existing practice is very low.

"The standards then carry none of your own reflection or thinking. They are not a summary statement of your own thinking through fundamental problems of what education should be for all children."

Politically, national standards without state and local involvement and refinement are not possible in a democracy. "In this country, we have to reinvent things in order to make them succeed," Secada reflects. "We are talking about fundamental shifts in our beliefs about children and what we think they need to learn. These shifts involve how we think about schooling in general. They will not succeed by simply saying we will adopt somebody else's thinking or statements."

Developing Local Standards

How should local districts proceed with their standards efforts to ensure that adequate and equitable input has been achieved? Are there particular individuals or community representatives they would be advised to include?

"The first constituency is obviously a selection of school personnel and parents," Secada responds. "In secondary schools, perhaps some students should be included, some union representation, and some of the affected stakeholders.

"This large group can break out into working groups as the process continues," he adds.

But simply inviting or appointing representatives from different constituencies is not sufficient, he points out. "There can be a tendency to believe that the committee is everything," he says, "but the committee needs to take the next step. It needs to actively seek the input of the constituencies that they represent and actively seek to educate those constituencies about what is at stake."

How might a committee engage in that process? Is there some sort of systematic method that might guarantee more success than another?

Secada believes that the process does not need to become overly mechanistic to educate and involve additional stakeholders. "Teachers go back to the schools and discuss what they're trying to do and why. Their job is to get their peers to reflect seriously on what they are doing."

Members of the community and parents can involve others through meetings of organizations such as the Lions Club, Secada suggests. "Again, the goal is to seek input and to give out information. Although it takes much longer to do things this way, it is the only way that really works. Committees typically get 6 months, but that is not nearly enough time."

He points to the 10 years that the National Council of Teachers of Mathematics (NCTM) needed to develop their standards for content and performance. "They began with a series of papers. They brought in groups from different constituencies. All of this took 10 years. The standards were sent to their membership for review and input. It was an incredibly democratic effort unmatched by any other."

Although 10 years might not be necessary, realistic time frames can't be circumvented, Secada maintains. "If we want broad citizen input, we have to be realistic about how long this process takes," he emphasizes.

The 10 years NCTM needed to develop its standards does not mean, he adds, that those standards are fixed and immutable. Instead, the organization currently is revising and updating the standards.

"This process of studying standards," Secada says, "is not trivial. If a community tries to write its own standards, they will encounter all sorts of obstacles. When they finally disseminate their standards, they will be the summary of a long effort that saw them enmeshed in serious problems."

How Many Standards?

If local communities and states continue to develop standards—as wise as that may be—is there a point where there are so many standards that they ultimately lack conviction or become meaningless? How might communities develop standards and avoid becoming mired in a tangle of standards that compete for attention—and end up never realized?

"There are already too many standards," Secada replies. "There is a 'me too' problem."

Another problem, one that is weightier, is that all standards are not created equally in terms of the intellectual rigor that goes into their development. "Many of these efforts are not thoughtful in the sense of broad domains of inquiry; they have not been subject to the kind of peer review and rigorous debate that is necessary."

The burgeoning of standards could be trimmed, Secada points out, if people were guided by the realization that not every content area needs standards. "We need to decide upon the core academic areas for which we want to have standards and limit them to those areas," he says.

But respect for constituencies who are invested in the development of standards that reflect their particular interests needs to be weighed, he adds. "The downside of these actions is that they make the standards movement top-heavy," he notes, "and makes it appear that we are bogged down in the construction of standards."

This concern, however, about the number and quality of standards can be translated into yet another positive incentive to spur public debate. "We may end up with the realization that these areas are important, but they are not central to the mission, Secada explains. This all becomes a part of the ongoing debate."

Expectations and Standards

When standards for content and performance are implemented in schools, should schools with a history of poor performance be treated more gently in being held accountable for results than are those with a track record of high academic achievement?

If so, does this suggest a two-tiered set of standards and expectations for schools?

To Secada, it is imperative that educators and the public realize that standards are not something fixed and static; rather, they are flexible goals toward which students continuously strive. Schools with a history of low student achievement could easily be discouraged from making such an effort—but instead, Secada insists that they engage in the process and set realistic timelines for action and results.

"There are various ways poor-performing schools could react to standards. Other than working to implement them, they could dismiss standards completely," he says. "They also might look at where they are and where they need to be. When they see this chasm, they could end up completely paralyzed."

Their accountability, he suggests, needs to be assessed in the longer term. "In 10 years, if these same schools haven't progressed, they have failed. They need to progress toward their goal, which should be to raise low achievement to a certain level. In order to do so, they need to configure their resources appropriately and make reasonable time commitments to realize high achievement."

Although scant progress can be explained, it cannot be excused, Secada asserts. "Now that we understand why we're not progressing, we need to work to change it. Do we become paralyzed or energized? Tough-minded self-assessment helps these schools bring about needed change."

And high-achieving schools, he concludes, should not rest on their laurels. "Schools that see themselves as reaching these standards should not become smug about their progress because there is always much more to do and to achieve."

4

Standards for
English Language Learners:
Deborah J. Short

Deborah J. Short is the Co-Director of the English Language and Multicultural Education division at the Center for Applied Linguistics (CAL) in Washington, DC. At CAL, she conducts research in the areas of English as a second language and bilingual education, specializing in the integration of language and content instruction in K-12 school settings. She provides professional development to school districts around the United States and also participates in curriculum and materials development projects.

At present, Short directs the national ESL Standards and Assessment Project for TESOL (Teachers of English to Speakers of Other Languages). In 1997, this project produced the ESL Standards for Pre-K–12 Students, *which is intended to help school personnel develop student proficiency in social and academic English and student sociocultural competence. Two companion documents, guidelines for assessing ESL students and a training manual for implementing the ESL standards, were published in March 1998.*

Deborah Short would not disagree with reformers who believe that rigorous, exacting standards for student content and performance should be high on the agendas of the nation and the states. She has just one, but considerable, caveat: For the most part, not taken into adequate account the needs of culturally and linguistically diverse students.

"All of these standards," Short begins, "include a statement that they are intended for all students, but when one examines the actual materials, they simply don't reflect all students.

"If the materials contain classroom vignettes or scenarios, there is seldom anything that relates to English language learners—with the exception of the English language arts standards. There is no discussion that provides information about what one should do if a student is learning English at the same time as science or mathematics."

Troubled by the implications of the standards movement for English language learners, TESOL leaders and members decided to produce standards specific to the needs of English language learners, developing standards, descriptors, progress indicators, and vignettes extracted from their own experience. "We were concerned as an organization and as a field that our students were being ignored," Short says.

"National standards are not equitable for English language learners," she continues. "But, on the other hand, content standards should be the same for all students. In other words, the goal for all students should be to reach the standards in mathematics, science, social studies, English, and language arts. But how do they get there? What's the best way to deliver instruction? To assess their learning? To provide time for them to meet these standards?"

These questions, she notes, represent a bramble patch that educators must negotiate, and it is complicated by the absence of a compelling research base to inform their decisions. "One of the most difficult issues facing schools and districts is how to integrate standards and, at the same time, work with students who aren't the average English-speaking students that we're used to serving in the schools. What accommodations are appropriate, both in terms of instruction and assessment? What time frames are appropriate? We don't have good research on this."

Myths and Misconceptions

Unfortunately, some school practices contribute to inequitable treatment of English language learners, particularly those that place English language learners in mainstreamed classes before their knowledge of English is sufficiently advanced, she argues. It is equally important to realize that popular perceptions of English language learners—although they grip the general public—are incorrect. One particularly persistent and pernicious belief about English language learners is that they are all the same, when actually there are tremendous variations between individuals and groups.

"There are English language learners," Short points out, "who have been well schooled in their native countries. After 2 years in the U.S., they're doing well. I can immediately think of a middle school in Silicon Valley where most students are children of Japanese, Korean, and Chinese engineers who work for the computer companies.

"These students," she adds, "enter school with very high academic competence. All they need to do is learn the English applicable to the content they already know. They receive a 2-year program which is very successful."

On the other hand, students from countries such as El Salvador—ravaged by war—may enter school in the United States actually illiterate or unschooled in their native language. "We may have a 13-year-old student who has had 2 years of formal schooling. To expect this person to reach the promotion standards necessary to move on to high school is simply not realistic."

Short poses a question. "I ask people if they would feel comfortable studying in a chemistry class taught in a foreign language after 3 years of that language in high school."

This, she believes, makes the intersection of content and language more immediate to people who are native English speakers. "Not only do students who come to the U.S. have to maintain the pace of their peers who are native English language speakers, but they have to catch up as well. Some may be at par in mathematics, but almost none are at par in U.S. history because they haven't studied it in their own countries."

She adds, "If they're studying the subject while they are also learning English, they are working doubly hard right from the start."

The consequences of such odds can be significant. "In Texas, for example, the Texas Assessment of Academic Skills includes an

English language proficiency test. School staff see an incredible amount of dropouts who see no way to pass the test and graduate from high school. Even if they stay in high school, there aren't alternate pathways or options."

Standards for English Language Learners

The ESL standards were developed to address the wide range of English language learners. They deliberately do not focus on long, specific lists but instead contain three broad goals. "These goals," Short adds, "reflect the three areas of language proficiency: social language, academic language, and sociocultural competence.

"Under each goal, we have three standards. These standards were designed so that a teacher could work on more than one standard in the same classroom."

But helping teachers understand these goals, she notes, is the crucial factor. "My perspective is that teachers are already doing much of what is specified. They may only have to make slight modifications or make more explicit connections."

In the training that TESOL has conducted, one exercise for teachers has been a reflection on a lesson that they taught recently that went well. "They write down a brief scenario that describes what they did and then compare that lesson to our set of standards and descriptors and ask, Did I meet any of these?"

Many teachers can see some relationship between their current practice and the TESOL standards, which Short says makes it easier from them to go forward. "Our approach to professional development is that teachers already have a lot of good knowledge and a lot of good skills. They may have to apply the activities they use in a slightly different way or be slightly more systematic or explicit about their connections to the standards, but this process should not be overwhelming."

The ESL standards are marked by aggressive professional development to ensure that teachers are prepared to make explicit those connections between content and acquisition of English. This development, Short explains, should begin in universities with programs of teacher education. "We are working on a book on teacher education intended to help teacher educators infuse the standards into some of the things they already do," she says. "If a college has a course on ESL methods, clearly, part of that course needs to talk about the standards-based instruction piece. We are trying to help faculty become more specific about the standards."

Potential teachers of English language learners need to learn much more than the principles and application of second language acquisition, she adds. "They need to learn that if they do certain things within the context of a specific lesson or activity, they are meeting a standard."

At the same time, Short and her colleagues would like to influence the fieldwork that teacher candidates must do as part of their preservice requirements. "If they are asked to go out and observe in classrooms, we're suggesting that the teachers ask them to reflect not just on the strategies they observe and how students react but also ask, How does this relate to standards? And as part of lesson designs that students might do as part of their student teaching, we are proposing some sample formats on how to do a lesson that includes standards."

Inservice professional development also receives a strong focus, she contends, ranging from curriculum development to the development of standards-based units to the development of assessments that match the standards. "Again, we emphasize many things that are practical, that can help teachers apply the standards or align the standards to their current curriculum."

This inservice professional development has been well received by those teachers who have taken part in it, she adds. "As a part of the training we give to trainers, we include materials on the conceptual framework, the theoretical foundation of the standards, their importance, why they are needed, curriculum development, assessment, sample syllabi that could be used in courses, and other sorts of materials that range from the theoretical to the practical."

Short says that the process of developing and implementing the ESL standards was informed by the development of the standards of other curriculum areas. "We tried to benefit as much as possible from other groups' processes," she notes. "We did not receive any federal funding or any supplemental funding. In fact, most of the standards were developed through lots of volunteer hours and the efforts of many, many members. TESOL and NABE [National Association of Bilingual Education] members from over 20 states participated in the writing and reviewing process.

"We were also committed to the dissemination of the standards," she continues.

Timeline for Implementation

Did the careful construction of the TESOL standards also include a timeline for implementation? What is realistic when educators embark upon such an ambitious effort?

"We have a few implementation sites," Short replies, "and we are documenting the process at those sites so we can share that information with other districts around the country that serve English language learners."

She points to technology as a key tool that will aid the dissemination and understanding of the ESL standards, particularly a database that will be placed on the World Wide Web. This database, she says, will provide an opportunity for different districts to share experiences and to network.

"We want to survey districts and provide information about their current status with the standards and what is available for people to see or talk about. For example, if you are a teacher in Nevada who suddenly has a new influx of ESL students—when you've only had two in the past 5 years in your school—and you want to do something that reflects the standards, is there another site like yours? Is there another district that recently had an influx of ESL students? What did they do? We believe that networking in this way will be the prime manner in which the implementation process will continue in the future."

Standards and Equity

The same concern for equity that nudged TESOL into developing the ESL standards informs the profession's belief that communities must be educated so that locally developed standards are just, reflecting the needs of all students. "A campaign is needed," she suggests, "almost like a public relations campaign, except this should be a campaign where the information presented to the public is based on research."

She adds, "We need to help people understand what it's like to be an English language learner. We should invite people to follow such a student for a day, to see what he or she struggles with on a daily basis. Or we might want to invite them to a chemistry class conducted in Italian."

Short emphasizes that the importance of English cannot be underestimated. "English diffuses all content areas in the classes that students take at school. You cannot progress in math, science, social studies, or health classes without knowing English. So for English language learners, the ESL standards are critical. They are not intended just for them to get their English/language arts credit but also to help them make that connection when they're sitting in the other content classrooms."

She also underscores that the immutability of some content areas, such as mathematics, does not hold for English language learners. Instead, their academic experience is fluid, elusive, and almost ephemeral. "If you walk into an eighth-grade math class," she points out, "for the most part, the curriculum and text are similar across the board. If you walk into an eighth-grade ESL class, eighth grade has little to do with the proficiency levels of the students."

The TESOL standards, Short contends, are certainly not an endpoint for the teachers of English language learners, and she cautions that they should not be considered in that light. "A metaphor that we have been using," she says, "is that native English-speaking students are on the education highway. They're traveling to a destination, which might be standards that they have to meet. They are traveling at a speed that may be 55 to 65 miles per hour."

In contrast, she portrays English language learners as motorists on secondary roads. "They may be moving parallel to the highway, but they're moving at slower speeds because they have all this baggage in their trunks.

"They're trying to catch up. They're trying to learn English, to learn the mainstream curricula. They simply can't go as fast. But we wanted to ensure that these students could not only learn English and the content areas but develop their understanding of the norms that govern how one uses English. We want to make sure they know the cultural conventions; how one addresses a teacher, how one addresses a peer.

"If we succeed," she concludes, "they can move up the exit ramp. When they reach the top, hopefully they can merge with all the other cars on the highway."

❖ 5 ❖

ESL Standards Enacted:
Maria Helena Malagón

Maria Helena Malagón is the Director of ESL/Bilingual Programs for the Montgomery County Public Schools in Montgomery County, Maryland, a position she has held for the past 15 years. She also has been an ESL teacher and a teacher specialist in ESL. She holds a master's degree in multicultural education from George Mason University. The Montgomery County Public Schools have been selected as a demonstration site for the implementation of the new ESL Standards developed by the TESOL (Teachers of English to Speakers of Other Languages) organization, which means that their progress will be documented and monitored by members of TESOL.

In the Montgomery County Public Schools, the challenges presented by English language learners are real and acute. Approximately 7,600 students (K-12) are enrolled in English as a Second Language (ESL), representing an almost dazzling array of 134 countries and 119 languages. The growth of this segment of the student population has been exponential and dramatic. In 1991, ESL students numbered 5,742. In 1998, they number 7,750—an increase of approximately 26%.

The number of English language learners classified as ESL students could easily result in confusion and competing goals—as could the sheer number of languages they speak. If varying levels of English language proficiency, socioeconomic status, and cultural differences are factored in, school staff could view their task as overwhelming. Instead, a new clarity has been brought to the ESL curriculum, as well as a sense of belonging within the schools' comprehensive academic program.

"In the mid-1990s," Malagón recollects, "Montgomery County began a large curriculum revision effort. In the ESL area, we felt very strongly that we needed to align what we were doing with the general education program, particularly in English, reading, and language arts."

The ESL program focused first on the beginning elementary curriculum. "We thought that level would be the easiest to revise," Malagón says, "and it was very much a trial-and-error process. But as time went on, we realized we needed to focus on middle school students as well."

The middle school level is one that Malagón finds especially critical, and one that is often overlooked by educators. "This group," she says, "has unique needs. Simply lumping them in with high school students and calling them secondary students wasn't good enough for us."

At the high school level, the same type of change is ongoing. "We are in the process," Malagón explains, "of modifying the intermediate curriculum for high school students. It is aligned to the English curriculum at the high school level; very similar to what we have done at the middle school, just not as far along with it."

As the county worked to revise and connect its curriculum to the regular academic curriculum, what concerns of ESL teachers and administrators had direct impact on changes that were made? "We felt it was time to provide uniformity across the county," Malagón responds. "If something is not in place, people begin to develop their own programs, often with little or no connection to anything else. We found that was happening.

"We also wanted to have clear expectations and clear standards for our students," she emphasizes.

In particular, ESL administrators wanted to edge away from a mentality in which English language learners were held to lower standards out of a sense of misguided pity. "We wanted instead to hold high standards for our kids and help them attain those standards,"

Malagón attests. "We didn't want different or lowered standards. We wanted the same standards for everybody."

Far too frequently, Malagón acknowledges, ESL teachers slip into an enabling mode with their students because they are aware of the difficulties their students face in school environments that often are uncaring or openly hostile to their needs. In addition, because many English language learners come from low socioeconomic backgrounds, school staff can perceive them as facing too many out-of-school obstacles to be able to succeed academically.

"Many ESL teachers," she says carefully, "have a desire to nurture and help their students, but sometimes they are caught in their own helpfulness. They don't realize that having a rigorous academic program is far better. A nurturing environment is absolutely necessary, but hand in hand come high expectations and high standards. The central question should be: How do we help kids reach these standards?"

Standards and Curriculum Revision

The Montgomery County Public Schools were careful to base their curriculum revision on the national standards developed by professional organizations in different content areas. But when the ESL program began its own curriculum revision, the ESL standards eventually developed by TESOL did not exist yet. As their own curriculum revision process progressed, the ESL standards were released, and MCPS staff were startled by the similarities.

Malagón explains, "At first, we only looked at a beginning elementary-level curriculum without looking at standards and outcomes. When we began working at the middle school level, we realized we needed to view this from the perspective of standards. By then, the ESL standards had been developed."

Although the ESL/TESOL standards were similar to their own work, the teachers in the ESL department in the Montgomery County Public Schools refined those standards to mesh with their own needs. Instead of three goals, as outlined in the ESL standards, they developed five goals, which they call outcomes. "They are very broad," Malagón explains, "but they combine the ESL standards with what we saw in the English standards and the reading and language arts standards. Admittedly, these are broad generic statements. We felt nobody could argue with them, and we hoped all kids could do them."

These five outcomes include statements that range from demonstrating a positive attitude toward using English in social and academic settings to demonstrating the ability to read, write, listen, and speak in English in a variety of forms and situations for a variety of purposes and audiences.

Becoming gradually more specific, the five outcomes flow into a series of benchmarks for student performance, such as "Students will communicate independently and collaboratively in English."

"These are still quite broad," Malagón says, "but as we developed our indicators, which was our next step, they became more specific."

After the indicators for student performance were developed—each falling under the five outcomes and benchmarks—hands-on instructional materials for teachers were devised, including teaching guides that had very specific activities for teachers.

Not only did the ESL program work to align its internal standards with those of the rest of the county, but it also recognized the need to be responsive to the increasing demands of state and local assessment programs. Aware that ESL students experience additional difficulties taking tests because of their level of English language proficiency—as well as test bias—part of the standards-based reform revolved around ensuring that students received adequate instruction in how to take tests and had an opportunity to practice test-taking skills.

"In much of the writing they do," Malagón explains, "they are given prompts to which they have to respond, because if they aren't taught to respond to prompts, they won't be able to take tests well. For instance, we might have them think of a time when somebody was very brave and explain what happened in writing."

Malagón continues, "If they have never encountered tests, they are not going to do well—so we do everything we can throughout our curriculum to make sure they will succeed."

Standards-Based Professional Development

How has the professional development matched MCPS's standards-based curricular reform? How has it been received by ESL staff? Have there been particular strategies that have proved particularly beneficial?

Malagón says that professional development has been conceptualized to meet the needs of ESL teachers at different levels. For example, during the 1997-1998 school year, elementary teachers have had monthly meetings with some focus on the new curriculum—but in the 1998-1999 school year, these meetings will focus completely on the changes.

To date, elementary ESL teachers have received an introduction to the ESL standards from TESOL representatives, with a focus on aligning the curriculum. "Alignment," Malagón emphasizes, "does not mean doing the same thing that everybody else does."

Instead, she maintains that alignment—in the best sense— means that ESL teachers are moving closer to the English curriculum and away from its previously isolated status. "By the time students are in the advanced level of ESL, materials should be shared, and we will instruct our students in similar skills. Clearly, a beginning ESL student is not going to be able to do the same things as a native English speaker in English class."

This alignment, Malagón contends, will converge ESL and English instruction at the advanced level. "We hope it will bring about an easier transition for students going from an ESL program into the regular education program."

But aside from the particular focus on curriculum alignment, the professional development for elementary-level ESL teachers is informed by presentations from different content levels—part of a systematic effort to connect the regular academic program with the ESL curriculum. "One month, we had the math coordinator speak about math," Malagón relates. "Of course, at the beginning, we had some people who didn't understand why they needed to learn about the math curriculum. However, he was able to make very clear links between math and language learning—emphasizing how language affects how successful students are in learning math."

She adds, "We've also had the reading/language arts coordinator, and have scheduled both social studies and science coordinators."

But she wants to emphasize that the staff development experienced by ESL teachers in the Montgomery County Public Schools is not limited to presentations or brief training sessions. "We plan to have focus groups at the different levels," she says, "which we have been doing with teachers at the middle school level who are field-testing the curriculum. We have found it to be very, very productive."

Focus groups, although perhaps unusual as a staff development activity, provide teachers with opportunities to share what works and refine what doesn't, she notes. These groups also serve as an opportunity to solicit teacher input into the changing curriculum in a way that is genuine.

"We have the entire curriculum on the computer," Malagón says, "and the teachers who are field-testing it are editing it and changing those things that didn't work. They also add things that they think are missing."

The 1998-1999 school year will expand to include all middle school teachers but with a different focus: feedback forums on each of the themes and activities in the curriculum. Malagón adds, "We also intend to provide plenty of opportunities for teachers to visit each other's classrooms. Focus groups will be a part of that as well."

The middle school teachers who are field-testing the new curriculum were deliberately chosen to reflect the entire county, she explains. "We have teachers from different geographic parts of the county. We have one teacher from a very large program; another with a smaller program. We have a first-year teacher and a very experienced teacher—and everything in between.

"We would like to discover if this curriculum works as well with a brand-new teacher as it does with a very experienced teacher. We are finding that it does."

In fact, Malagón admits to some surprise that the teachers most interested in the standards-based ESL curriculum are new teachers and very experienced teachers. "Others are excited about it, but we do see the most excitement in those two teacher groups."

Developing an Integrated Curriculum

The key is connecting to the rest of the curriculum, Malagón says emphatically. "We don't want English language learners to experience an isolated curriculum."

English language learners traditionally have been isolated from the rest of the school, she adds—a practice that does not facilitate their emergence as successful students. "In the 1970s and early 1980s," Malagón explains, "ESL tended to operate without much connection between what went on in other classrooms. Now we work with administrators and principals to get schools, particularly at the elementary level, to schedule ESL classes at the same time as reading/language arts."

The benefits are clear, she believes, and can be seen in cooperative, collegial work between ESL teachers and English teachers. ESL teachers work on the same kinds of skills as reading/language arts teachers, but at a level appropriate for students' English language skills.

The final piece, one that Malagón is especially excited about, is the opportunity—and the mandate—for ESL teachers and regular classroom teachers to engage in joint planning and reach an increased awareness of each other's instruction.

Although this new emphasis in professional development at first met with resistance, Malagón reports that middle school teachers in particular, who have been field-testing the revised curriculum, have been especially receptive to it. "They are promoting the curriculum to their peers and creating an excitement about it," she says. "At this point, we have four teachers field-testing it, but next year we are going to a countywide pilot."

Chief benefits, she observes, to participating teachers include the fact that they have a framework that simultaneously encourages creativity. "At our last meeting, teachers were discussing what they were working on, and they were working on the same things but doing it differently. They agreed that if any of their students had gone to another teacher's class, that student would have been absorbed immediately because the skills and language that were being taught were all the same."

Standards and Previous Practice

Part of the reason that the new standards-based curriculum has been received enthusiastically by teachers is that connections to what they did previously have been made explicit. "When we first presented the standards to teachers," Malagón says, "we told them we had organized a lot of things we already had been doing. We were careful to present the material in a fashion that was user-friendly."

She describes the middle school curriculum and how it was introduced. "We provide an introduction to the curriculum, its philosophy, how we teach structure, how we teach vocabulary, those sorts of things."

New additions were culture and assessment, Malagón points out. "We also added an overview. All of this is organized by theme. We calculated that each theme takes about 9 weeks to teach."

The themes connect to themes in the English curriculum, she says, explaining that the ESL curriculum differs from the regular curriculum in that it is based on language proficiency instead of grade level. As she says, "We don't have a separate curriculum for sixth, seventh, or eighth grade. Instead, we have a middle school curriculum, but it is based on beginning, intermediate, and advanced levels of language proficiency. We combine what we see in the sixth-, seventh-, and eighth-grade English program and incorporate it into ours."

Within each theme are "essential questions" that must be answered by students during the 9 weeks. "As an example of essential questions," Malagón explains, "one of the things we focus on is Hopes and Dreams, which, in the English curriculum, is called Vision Quests. Our essential questions, just as an example, within that theme include: Who are you? What are your cultural roots? What are your goals? How do you plan to reach them?

"We then go into common tasks, such as: Read a biography or an autobiography. Write a personal goal statement that includes your long-term goals, what you have to do to achieve your goals, and what you can do this year to make your dream possible. The final common task is for each student to write his or her autobiography."

Theme I: Hopes and Dreams

Essential Questions

1. Who are you, and what are your cultural roots?
2. What are your goals, and how do you reach them?

Common Tasks

1. Read a biography or an autobiography or a biography of a fictional character.
2. Write a personal goals statement:
   What are your long-term goals?
   What do you have to do to achieve your goals?
   What can you do this year to make your dream possible?
3. Write an autobiography.

Language Focus

1. Simple past tense
2. Past tense
3. Sequencing
4. Transition words
5. Capitalization and punctuation

Anchor Text

All Star English, Student Book 2, pp. 63-82, and *All Star English, Book 2*, Skills Journal A, pp. 63-82.

Note: Excerpted from Montgomery County Public Schools ESL Curriculum for Middle School Students.

Exhibit 5.1. An Example of Montgomery County Public Schools ESL Curriculum: Thematic Illustration

The results of such assignments and prompts, Malagón says, "were powerful. We see where kids already are and tap into that knowledge to build upon it."

Instructional Goal 1:
Introduce the Hopes and Dreams Theme
and Essential Questions

Sample Activities and Assessments

1. Read "Hi! My Name is Carmen." (*Student Book 3*, pp. 4-6 and corresponding skills pages)
2. Write five questions and use them to interview a classmate, take notes, and introduce your classmate.
3. Post or distribute copies of essential questions. Who are you, and what are your cultural roots? What are your goals, and how do you reach them?

Instructional Goal 2:
Develop the Concept of Cultural Roots

Sample Activities and Assessments

1. List all the words that come to mind when you say "America" (small-group activity).
2. Each student completes a tree about himself/herself.
3. View films such as *Molly's Pilgrim, Welcome to Miami Cubanos, Overture: Linh From Vietnam, Unicorn in the Garden, Jade Snow,* and *The Three Worlds of Maria Gutierrez* in terms of both essential questions.

Exhibit 5.2. Examples of Montgomery County Public Schools ESL Instructional Goals

The curriculum is carefully crafted to include instructional goals for each theme that relate to the essential questions, including sample activities, a selection of films, and discussion questions to guide teachers. "We also can draw in our bilingual counseling component," she says, "because the topics addressed by our counselors complement the themes in the curriculum."

Instructional Goal 3:
Introduce and Discuss the Autobiography,
Biography, and Writing Prompts

Sample Activities and Assessments

1. Listen to one or two short biographies from sources such as *People Magazine, Mini-Page,* encyclopedias, or obituaries. While the teacher is reading, students listen for tense and remember examples from the text when they recognized the past tense.
2. Listen again. Create a live timeline based on events contributed by students. Write the timeline. Compare to the text. How is it the same? How is it different? Insert transition words in the timeline by inserting teacher-made laminated cards.

Note: Excerpted from the Montgomery County Public Schools ESL Curriculum for Middle School Students.

Exhibit 5.2., Continued. Examples of Montgomery County Public Schools ESL Instructional Goals

The connection to the rest of the school is already apparent, Malagón says, and is illustrated through one teacher's experience with a student. "The student came into her class and said, 'This is just like an English class!'"

To Malagón and her colleagues, this is high praise, because it helps legitimize the ESL curriculum.

She emphasizes that although all writing and other activities are conducted in English, students are not left to flounder. "We always provide a prompt, and we build off an activity or exercise they have already done. For example, at the middle school level, we ask, Imagine you have been asked to write an article for the school newspaper about the famous person you recently discussed in class. Before you begin to write, think about where and when the person was born, some important event in the person's life, and the person's goals and achievements. Now write an article for the school newspaper about this person."

This prompt, she states, helps students structure their work yet allows creativity.

Reflections on Change

Which changes have been the most significant since the Montgomery County Public Schools have moved districtwide to standards-based curricula? Which changes, in particular, mark the ESL program area?

Malagón believes that clear goals and outcomes distinguish the change more than any other factors. As she says, "Teachers now have a clear sense of where they want to take their kids. They also have a systematic way to go about this. At least, this is what they tell us. They spend just as much time planning, but they plan in a much more creative manner. They say they enjoy it much more because it goes beyond, 'What do I do tomorrow?'

"They have a road map," she adds, "and they have the freedom, along with the structure, to take their students where they need to go."

References and Selected Bibliography

References

Apple, M. W. (1993). The politics of official knowledge: Does a national curriculum make sense? *Teachers College Record, 95,* 222-241.

Berliner, D. C., & Biddle, B. J. (1996, May). Standards amidst uncertainty and inequality. *School Administrator, 53,* 42-44+.

Boyer, E. L. (1983). *High school: A report on secondary education in America/The Carnegie Foundation for the Advancement of Teaching.* New York: Harper & Row.

Carnegie Forum on Education and the Economy Task Force on Teaching as a Profession. (1986). *A nation prepared: Teachers for the 21st century: The report of the Task Force on Teaching as a Profession, Carnegie Forum on Education and the Economy.* Washington, DC: Author.

Holmes Group. (1986). *Tomorrow's teachers: A report of the Holmes Group.* East Lansing, MI: Author.

Kendall, J. S., & Marzano, R. J. (1997). *Content knowledge: A compendium of standards and benchmarks for K-12 education* (2nd ed.). Aurora, CO: McREL; and Alexandria, VA: ASCD.

Meier, D. (1989). National standards for American education. *Teachers College Record, 91,* 25-27.

National Center for Education Statistics. (1998). *A study of twelfth-grade mathematics and science achievement in international context.* Washington, DC: Author.

National Commission for Excellence in Teacher Education. (1985). *A call for change in teacher education.* Washington, DC: Author.

National Commission on Excellence in Education. (1983). *Meeting the challenge: Recent efforts to improve education across the nation: A report to the Secretary of Education/prepared by the staff of the National Commission on Excellence in Education.* Washington, DC: U.S. Department of Education.

National Commission on Excellence in Education. (1984). *A nation at risk: The imperative for educational reform: A report to the nation and the Secretary of Education, United States Department of Education/by the National Commission on Excellence in Education.* Washington, DC: U.S. Department of Education.

Ravitch, D. (1995). *National standards in American education: A citizen's guide.* New York: Brookings Institution.

Smith, M. S., Fuhrman, S. H., & O'Day, J. A. (1994). National curriculum standards: Are they desirable and feasible? In *Yearbook of the Association for Supervision and Curriculum Development* (pp. 12-29). Reston, VA: ASCD.

Smith, M. S., Stevenson, D. L., & Li, C. P. (1998, March). Voluntary national tests would improve education. *Educational Leadership,* pp. 42-44.

Selected Bibliography

Burrill, G. (1997, October). The NCTM standards: Eight years later. *School Science and Mathematics,* pp. 335-339.

Cobb, N. (Ed.). (1995). *The future of education: Perspectives on national standards in America.* New York: College Board.

Darling-Hammond, L. (1994). National standards and assessments: Will they improve education? *American Journal of Education, 102,* 478-510.

Gagnon, P. A. (1994). The case for standards: Equity and competence. *Journal of Education, 176*(3), 1-16.

Hershberg, T. (1997, December 10). The case for new standards in education. *Education Week, 17,* 52+.

Howe, K. R. (1994, November). Standards, assessment, and equality of educational opportunity. *Educational Researcher, 23,* 27-33.

Louis, K., & Versloot, B. (1996). High standards and cultural diversity: Cautionary tales of comparative research—a comment on "Benchmarking education standards" by Lauren B. Resnick, Katherine J. Nolan, and Daniel P. Resnick. *Educational Evaluation & Policy Analysis, 18,* 253-261.

McKeon, D. (1994, May). When meeting "common" standards is uncommonly difficult. *Educational Leadership, 51,* 45-49.

National Council of Teachers of Mathematics/Commission on Standards for School Mathematics. (1989). *Curriculum and evaluation standards for school mathematics.* Reston, VA: Author.

Noddings, N. (1997, November). Thinking about standards. *Phi Delta Kappan, 79,* 184-189.

Porter, A. (1995, January/February). The uses and misuses of opportunity-to-learn standards. *Educational Researcher,* pp. 21-27.

Ravitch, D. (1993, June). Launching a revolution in standards and assessments. *Phi Delta Kappan, 74,* 767-772.

Reigeluth, C. M. (1997, November). Educational standards: To standardize or customize learning? *Phi Delta Kappan, 79,* 202-206.

Resnick, L. B., & Nolan, K. J. (1995, March). Where in the world are world-class standards? *Educational Leadership, 52,* 6-10.

Resnick, L. B., & Wirt, J. G. (Eds.). (1996). *Linking school and work: Roles for standards and assessment.* San Francisco: Jossey-Bass.

Romberg, T. A. (1993, February). NCTM's standards: A rallying flag for mathematics teachers. *Educational Leadership, 50,* 36-41.

Rose, M. (1994, April). Working toward world-class standards. *American Teacher, 78,* 9-12.

Shanker, A. (1993, Summer). Can we meet world-class standards? *American Teacher, 78,* 7.

Tucker, M., & Codding, J. B. (1998). *Standards for our schools: How to set them, measure them, and reach them.* New York: Simon & Schuster.

CORWIN
PRESS

The Corwin Press logo—a raven striding across an open book—represents the happy union of courage and learning. We are a professional-level publisher of books and journals for K-12 educators, and we are committed to creating and providing resources that embody these qualities. Corwin's motto is "Success for All Learners."

DATE DUE